Mental Health and VSHS Prayer Therapy

The Move to New Earth

VERONIQUÉ SALAGEAN

You are immune to it until in a moment of self-reflection, when through some calculation you decouple and realise what is hidden inside you: your traumas, disorders, illnesses and any type of demonic influence. Of course, there are an infinite number of variations to get to that point. I know for a fact, this blueprint that I am presenting in this book, you can make the move to the New Earth because these modalities are universal and designed for our entire system functionality.

CONTENTS

1.   INTRO

Hello There,

This magnificent my second self-help book is dedicated to people for making their move into the New World, New Earth. It all came about after I've written and published 'CHANGE YOUR LIFE: with Practical Techniques' when my Intuition which I believe to be identical with the Divine Power, God, Source was keep telling me to write such a book dedicated only to the removal of all that is negativity. So, what I will do in this book is to present to you my actual blueprint of the move to New World, New Earth. Only suggesting, but you should take this information as many will and have already followed this highway since it is the only fastest way.

Before we start, please know that this book is written from My Higher Self, no Ego involved but in my own specific style of writing, straight to the point and solutions. I will use my personal case study as an example for you to follow or at least try it especially when your life gets out of control. Otherwise, this book will contribute to your universal knowledge or at least to your awareness and clarity. The VSHS Prayer Therapy technique is transferred from my beloved first self-help book 'CHANGE YOUR LIFE: with Practical Techniques'.

Please be patient in reading this book as I do live an intense life, my experiences have overlapped although I will try to keep it clear and for you to understand how all unfolded. I will also try to shrink as much information as possible and keep it simple. The starting point is a story of searching. In my case it's been over and over again the feeling of Unhappiness that made me take drastic turns. Love made me reach where I am today, move mountains but in search of finding my True Happiness which all fuelled the 'keep going' and 'don't look back!'

I would like to Thank You to all the people that contributed their part in reaching where I am today. I would like to Thank You to my incredible soul, it is an honour and inspiration to have it. My parents that I've chosen and genetic lineages for the overall beauty, strength and power. Since I was a child, I struggled feeling part of my family, struggled feeling at home here on Planet Earth and I am glad I didn't have the power and courage to actually take my life a few times. It has been until today, 25 December 2025 a truly remarkable journey that I never thought to feel so blessed, special and unique in the most humble and appreciative way. I also Thank You to God that after losing myself I

accepted and embraced it back into my life as
Faith, Source and seriously believing and
collaborating with The Universe (even going in the
park and talking with it, with voice towards the sky).

I suggest you to focus on your personal life change
if truly interested, take notes, study this course with
highlighter pen and *apply the techniques **EXACTLY
as I say***.

Thank you for your trust and I will see you in the
next chapter.

<u>NOTE</u>: For anyone narrow minded and immature or
judgmental, I sincerely declare I don't care who
thinks of me or about me. I cordially own my life,
choices and decisions and I regret nothing, but
benefited all along if analysing my life progression.
So, I Don't Really Care. If you are collaborating with
any type of magic and happy with it, this book might
be irrelevant to you but 100% can make you move
into the New Earth (where there is abundance,
divine energy and not manipulation and stealing).

2. THE BLUEPRINT

A long story short, it all started for me about 6 years ago when I've been having moments of switching off preferences and moments of sudden likes change. Then, Covid-19 hit and during the pandemic I've taken a strong decision to Quiet The Mind technique of strict regime, every day a few times. Sometimes on the days of 'what to do?' I've been Quieting The Mind 3-4 times a day for a minimum of 20 minutes each session. Just sitting in Buddha posture or seated in silence, thinking Nothing in my big majestic vintage green leather armchair. I really had days and days and days and moments when I didn't see the light at the end of the tunnel. I was coming out of the session and thinking to myself 'Where is all this heading?' - this is because the Ego needed to know as was becoming scared of the uncertainty. My Higher Self knew exactly what was happening and kept telling me through the Intuition 'You will see, it's going to be sooo good when you get there. Just a bit more patience. Patience, Patience, a bit more Patience.' Then there were days I was getting frustrated, days where people reacted towards me. And because, after studying it, I've realised the system started to calibrate and organise. Therefore, the mind and whole system (energetic system) purifies and becomes at peace, the inner world becomes harmonious. As a side note, when you are within these natural techniques of such power, there is a probability your issues will be presented to you by someone (with me it always happened in the society from strangers so I could see clearly what is happening in my life). With the VSHS Prayer Therapy is the same but first it was showing to me in the dream and what is all about. So, when someone reached in an unpleasant way towards me, I knew the issue was getting out of my system (These situations happened not all the time, but rarely). **Just trust you are safe and do not react to these situations - is just your system clearing! Keep and set your mind and yourself into Relax Mode.**

Moreover, the pandemic was coming to an end. And just before that, I've decided to listen to my Intuition and follow the impulses of its guidance: to search the internet.

At first, I bumped into KAP by Venant Wong and then Bruce Lipton popped up on my YouTube timeline talking about Psych-K modality (I remember, I didn't know who he was at that time, only after that I've documented him.) Immediately I've searched and greatly informed about these two modalities. Searched for the KAP facilitators here in London and practitioners of Psych-K (someone close to my residency). Thanks to the beautiful Internet, I've found my people instantly, and took the decision to try KAP first and then Psych-K. My

Intuition picked the KAP facilitator for me and also the Psych-K practitioner. When I say Intuition, I mean that gut instinct, inner voice that insists on one information to be accepted. As a side note, these were all signs for changing my life a bit more.

By the way, words can't describe what The Quiet Mind technique does. Although, it is very wordy presented by Abraham Hicks and very few of their followers have reaped the benefits and rewards. (Well, this is humanity nowadays, just disconnected from Divinity. Now I understand - then I didn't, why Abraham Hicks loses its patience as people are not listening as practicing the technique. (Yes! They are Hearing but not Listening!) So, I was Quieting The Mind in an intense regime for 6 months and then started slowing down the numbers of sessions per week (I was doing it when I felt needed).

Furthermore, I booked and went to a semi-private KAP session of only 4,5 participants with Phillippa Gail. By the way, I've recorded all my aftermath sessions as I've found the sessions so fascinating, out of this world. I expected nothing from it, just my Intuition told me to do it and I fully trusted it without doubt. I always knew my Intuition wants my best as it helped and saved me from troubles all my life.

About Kundalini, I would say about 9 years ago of today's year 2025, I've listened to some meditations of its awakening. I've done it a few times at home and each time was feeling a heavy pain that I couldn't take it at the bottom of my spine. So, I completely stopped practicing with myself in a Buddha seated posture listening to Kundalini Awakenings. After this, about a year later I would say, I found the man that I've been searching for all my life and didn't know why. My very first Past Life Regression session with Nicolas Aujula was about finding out 'Why I've searched for this man all my life?' as then now I knew who he was, how he looked and his name. Finding Nicolas Aujula prior to Pandemic, has been the same Intuition impulse, guidance and practitioner chosen.

As a side note, at that time I was visiting a clairvoyant / psychic (now I don't recommend it, I was naive and inexperienced at that time, please understand!). You see, what I've discovered, clairvoyants / psychics / white angels worshipers collaborate with spirits that even themselves don't know what exactly these entities are and what they are collaborating with or inviting in (I call this white magic or unrested souls that are cursed - and Why? Because I've been a commodity to them and reflected numerous bad luck situations in my life). Anyhow, I was also keeping in touch with a gifted tarot reader at the same time (two different people, in two different countries and languages, one English, the other Spanish). Both these ladies pointed in the same direction as I've been searching for Him everywhere for so many years. Even came to London searching for him and knew he was here as I was landing. I knew I would find him here. And I did!

To conclude this, I've met a few times by coincidence Mr. DF here in London at his workplace (retail manager at major shopping stores) and we came more and more closer as a soul connection. One afternoon at home, returning from our store encounter, I felt tired so I took a nap. This afternoon I had my first Kundalini awakening and experience. I am certain what could cause it was the soul link with Mr. DF since probably we were twin flames (now reflecting back). As you can imagine, I had a very strong soul connection with him. The dreaming that afternoon was vivid and I believe it was when my ability to see within the dream the betrayal or cheating of my beloved partner, it was unlocked.

Moreover, I had a few more awakenings in the afternoon during naps before Covid-19. Absolutely fascinating experiences and perhaps there was a contribution from Nicolas Aujula since he said he had his Kundalini already awakened. I remember, sharing with Nicolas Aujula about this awakening of mine and saying that it doesn't rise higher than to the Heart Chakra. And I've been having lots of resistance to allow it to transcend to the head.

Now back to KAP, this is what I've shared with Phillippa about my Kundalini experience: It was awakening by itself but it was not passing through the Heart Chakra. I didn't know the reason but I knew something was wrong within my system. I would say I had about 6 awakenings over the years until the first session of KAP in July 2022. Now, I won't go into much details about my sessions as I planned to write a book specifically about my Kundalini. But, I've discovered through the sessions, the big accumulation and carrying a LOT of suffering (this is the great damage created from my mom's relationship towards me over 25 years). 3 KAP sessions later on of not moving at all but coming out from each session unstoppably of extreme crying and suffering for an hour or two. Felt very quiet, something detached from me (the comforting feeling of holding into love suffering and pain was slowly removing from my system). It felt like something was ripped from my reality and I was feeling down for a few days after each session. On the 4th KAP session I had the actual full Kundalini awakening out of the body experience. Right from the first day afterwards I felt the Oneness, a very strong and settled feeling of All being, as if I was part of each object, molecule and everything in the entire Cosmos. I strongly felt omnipresent and co-existing everywhere. An absolutely incredible feeling! All positive.

Here is what I was trying to illustrate with KAP by Venant Wong and going to Phillippa Gail sessions, only with her since I believed she was truly gifted with it. For all the old souls that are holding into or had accumulated low vibration energy into their system or being holded back from their true potential, KAP saved my life. I've been and am very grateful to Venant Wong for creating KAP as otherwise God knows when would've managed to travel to India for my Heart Chakra unblocking (certainly, I would've delayed for myself the unconditional love living). Yes, my material cord was instantly and permanently cut within this 4th session although now after two years I returned back to the material world in a fine way. As Phillippa said it 'the Kundalini energy has greatly balanced within the energy field'.

Certainly, life with Kundalini is very zen and I still think I have a material life purpose to fulfill. Therefore, even to travel the world I needed money, and then I still enjoyed luxury. For me personally, Zen living was fine for a few months until I got bored and passed over the illusion, delusion, quantum jumping and asking myself 'Am I mad, losing my mind?' I recounted Phillippa: 'The snail was there on my porch, next to me a minute ago, then when I looked back at it, it was not there anymore, it disappeared!' This was only one experience within many others. I really thought I was losing my mind, because the world around me, this world was all feeling unreal and an illusion. (Only people with positive Kundalini experiences or high in spirituality will understand my phenomena). My life with Kundalini was a fun journey of rediscovering the World for what actually is - an Illusion in motion.

Sincerely, I don't regret KAP or my awakening. I recommend it if your Intuition tells you to do it. Or at least try it as it is designed to contribute to your well-being. **Listen and trust your Intuition. But I do recommend it as it has done so much good to my system, no harm at all.**

Just as a side note, I've bumped into some website's reviews talking, some talking rubbish about Kundalini awakening meetings and here and there and in India. Well, I would say **We Attract Who We Are!** So, if you or anyone met rubbish people at Kundalini sessions, it is because they forced its energy from the base (KAP is the opposite, the energy drops from the top of the head travelling down into the energy system, clearing your energy blockages and without forcing anything). Therefore, it seems to me there is a Kundalini society of two levels, lower and higher (Higher, us the positive ones). By the way, Who are you to point out, when you are exactly the same?

I've met lovely people at KAP sessions. Nobody had corrupted minds, negative, living in hell, crazy and on drugs. So, what are some people talking about?

Moving on, I've chosen Eylem Govtepe for my Psych-K sessions. Eylem has been incredibly supportive and helpful in my desire to change my life and my mindset. I've done two sets of 3 sessions each with Eylem and at the end of it a few months later felt I actually changed my parents. Collaborating with Eylem has been a true life change because I believed in her and trusted her so to have a life makeover. Two years later, after a set of 9 days of prayer at 6AM in my bathroom towards the East, my Intuition took me back to Psych-K to fully complete more of my New Paradigm.

To conclude, from March 2020 to December 2024 so many things have taken place, changes, challenges for me, towards me that I just didn't complain or resist. But, working with each of what was thrown at me. I kind of knew that there was and from where was originating everything - My childhood. I had to find the beginning of each story and change that beginning. So, I paid and I got fixed because we live in an advanced and information era and there are gifted people ready to help and support you - Just search. I have a saying: **'Who Searches Finds!'**

My full Kundalini awakening with KAP happened within 3 months and Psych-K I've managed within the following 4 months. On the first day of January 2023 I had a complete new turn.

This turn has led me to newly transform and now in 2025 the paradigm of my Destiny will change according to my personalised Vedic astrology report.

The VSHS Prayer Therapy (Veroniqué Salagean Higher Self Prayer Therapy) was born from my experience with being a target and commodity to white magic for a few months from the first day of January 2023. The story of it can be found in my other book 'CHANGE YOUR LIFE: with Practical Techniques'.

Therefore, in this book I will be focusing on the reaping benefits of doing the VSHS Prayer Therapy since I am unsure of what will happen with the people of soon to become in 2025, The Old Earth. I mean, dying is one thing but overcoming the challenges but transitioning to the New Earth is this book's knowledge. If these people remain alive for a few years, I don't think it will be an easy living if I have to reflect on my year 2024. For me, Year 2024 has been the most challenging and intense year of my life. People, experiences and a mind blowing manifestation have been thrown at me. I've kept myself in strong communication with my Intuition, constantly self-reflecting, self-talking, self-empowering into my Power and Strength and yet I found it: 'get me out of this year'. I was 12 nights before its end, and was starting eagerly counting down towards 2025.

To now conclude everything, if you want to change your life and make the move into the New Earth I suggest my blueprint. I believe some of the old or very old souls have died in the Covid-19 process. I am unsure what will happen to the old souls left out, someone like me, old soul, perhaps very old souls passed healthily through Covid-19.

Most probably with question mark, the Covid-19 deaths will be returning to the New Earth and go through these modalities since we all leave our pains and troubles here. As Dolores Cannon said from the universal reports, we must finish the Earth's School before graduating. I believe that after graduating from the Earth's School only then will we be allowed to try new experiences in new Planets, Worlds, Galaxies. I also believe that old souls, very old souls returning to Planet Earth into the New Earth's frequency, they most probably will return into these modalities as a life purpose to fulfill so for them to graduate Earth's School. Well, I said many things and predicted and many turned out to be true. So, whatever the outcome is from the Year 2025 as per astrological predictions, planet's alignments and the two worlds separating

will be more obviously seen after years have
passed and looking backwards to connect the dots.

Anyhow,

KAP by Venant Wong, **Psych-K by Rob Williams**, **VSHS Prayer Therapy by Veroniqué Salagean** and **QHHT by Dolores Cannon** are that form the complete blueprint to the move to New Earth, New World as for an old, very old soul. Also, I am very sure the New Earth's frequency will force people to listen to their Intuition and take impulsive guidance towards these modalities that are enlightening. They all give miracles, are natural and give life change results. If you would like to find information about anything personal, a Past Life Regression session can help although QHHT does the same but with an extra part for Health Healing (accessing your Higher Self).

3.   THE MOVE TO NEW EARTH

Now, here we start with the actual beautiful beginning.

After taking out from my all past lives, genetic lineage, whole system, space, mind and life all the traumas one by one (a VSHS Prayer Therapy of one issue/disorder every three days, where I prayed for at least 300 times of Faith and Kneeling in 2024 in my bathroom facing East) , all the issues, any possible mental, emotional, personality disorders and illnesses - I arrived on time for the Planet Earth decoupling. So, I did make the move into the New Earth. And how do I know it? - I am feeling light, happier, much more confident, powerful and with an inner sense of fulfillment. Also I've stopped being in a rush to a deadline.

Now, let's remember that in the beginning of the year 2023 I kept saying 'I don't know why, but I have to rush, I have to arrive on time. I don't have time!' x 3, 4 times. I even told an acquaintance these words and felt in a real hurry and as if I don't have time anymore as if something is coming up.

Although, I kept looking into it and saw nothing of death or my life actually ending. But it simply didn't make sense. And, did I make it on time? Ohh Yesss.

Some say, it is the move from Ground and Water to Air and Fire which I totally believe. Well, we know traditionally Kundalini represents the Fire of burning Karma and the old patterns within the energy system. Air represents consciousness, expansion, becoming mindfulness and open-minded - recognising *Everything has a beginning, a Source, a Starting Point.* I have proven myself this over and over again from the VSHS Prayer Therapy since I was dreaming vividly where the issue comes from and people involved. The 'Intro' chapter of CHANGE YOUR LIFE: with Practical Techniques gives the story of how it all unfolded for me.

Nevertheless, VSHS Prayer Therapy is an advanced therapy that you do with yourself. QHHT is quite similar for accessing your Higher Self. VSHS Prayer Therapy does an incredible job, is natural but done with the help of your Higher Self, with the power of your Spirit and with your power of Faith - Just believe in it, in this technique! It works wonders! Then, what you will most probably do otherwise, I strongly suggest is to **cross by airplane the water patch** to some destination, perhaps going on a holiday. I recommend doing this *every 6 months* so your energy system updates to the changes made. It simply upgrades! Eylem told me about Crossing the water by airplane and how it disconnects and cuts cords of energy (she knows it from her studies). Anyhow, what I've found to be true, it updates your entire system from the VSHS Prayer Therapy.

In addition to this, the demonic influence (Extreme Fear and others) that I had, not only on the financial side but also on the people's side, I removed through a different method.

Something beautiful happened to me carrying on with the VSHS Script Letter Technique (you can find this technique into my CHANGE YOUR LIFE: with Practical Techniques book) and in combination with the VSHS Prayer Therapy - it led me to a Spotify Channel of a pastor's prayers. These two types of prayers have been designed to take out from your life any demonic hindrances and influence of financials and people (two different prayers).

What I've done, I've written them on paper (since they were a few minutes long) and recorded them at a slow pace, each. At 2:59 AM I kneeled in my bathroom, took three breaths in and out (same procedure as for the VSHS Prayer Therapy) and I started reciting at 3AM the prayer from my personal recording. I've prayed for *each prayer 3 days in a row at 3AM.*

How did I know about my demonic influence? In the moment of praying I had very strong waves of sweat, fear, a sense of someone was looking behind me and around me, also a strong feeling of fainting and losing strength and power. At some point, I was feeling so weak that I had to kneel seated from kneeling upright posture. But I was so determined and didn't stop praying even though I was feeling that way. The demonic influence on the financial side was very very very strong. I can't explain to you the dream I had - absolutely incredible! It actually worked wonders with this Jesus Christ prayer! (You can watch the movie 'Puss in Boots: The Last Wish' to understand more or less what happened in my dream as he was confronting his fear, demonic influence in his dream).

In the dream of the prayer regarding Life, it showed me the people that I depended on and someone from my childhood. Later on, after meeting these people, I've realised that they have been removed from my life and the connection to them permanently cut without affecting my great rapport with them. Absolutely incredible! It simply worked!

Therefore, after removing these demonic influences that I was keeping myself, years after years from reaching my financial potential and people constantly using me, the upcoming 2025 astrological Vedic report prediction is that my own destiny's paradigm changes. I mean, of course, I contributed to what is coming up for me!

The Spotify channel that I found it is called:
BEYOND GRACE PRAYER PODCAST

You can search it, otherwise pastors can provide these greatly formulated prayers with the specific purpose of removing the demonic influence, demonic hindrances out of your system. Therefore, it can be done. Where there is a will, is a way!

But, anyhow allow me to help you a bit more as for sharing with you the prayers I actually used for these two matters. I suggest you record them on your phone at a slow pace for morning reciting. I must admit, praying at 3AM is truly challenging! I don't know what it actually is, but the numbers 3, 6, and 9 have a powerful cosmic vibration.

So, set the alarm a bit earlier, perhaps 2:50AM, time yourself well. If you feel like drinking some water or eating, it simply doesn't affect the prayer. You will go in the bathroom, close the toilet then close the bathroom door. Lay down a folded clean towel, I use white colour. Kneeling at 2:59 AM towards the East or corner (not towards the toilet or door) , take 3 breaths IN through the nose and OUT through the mouth. At 3AM you will start saying the prayer with a low tone voice as you are listening to it from the recording.

Remember, if you give up praying, you will have to restart all over again. I suggest making the decision and strong commitment for its completion. I personally don't regret doing it and free myself from the unfavourable influence. I had enough of so many years of mental and emotional abuse and also financial struggle. These are the prayers:

3 days: 3AM Prayer for Finances

God, I come before you today, seeking breakthroughs in my finances.

Thank you for being faithful and true to your promises. I believe you are going to give me the resources and favour I need to break through this financial struggle. I come to you because you are God, my provider. I know you will supply all my needs according to your riches in Christ Jesus. God, please create an opening of your abandoned Supernatural Supply, break every curse of poverty and lack my life. Break, open the gates of heaven and pour out your blessings upon me. Rebuke the devourer against my finances for my sake. Your word in Joel chapter 2 verses 24 to 26, says that "the threshing floors will be filled with grain. The Vats will overflow with new wine and oil. I will repay you for the years the locust has eaten, the great locust and the young locust. You will have plenty to eat until you are full and you will praise the name of the Lord your God who has worked wonders for you. Never again, will my people be shamed. Take me from financial loss to financial increase in Jesus name.

I pray to God that he will send defined connections, resources and opportunities the way that merits me financially.
I pray that the blessings of God chase and overtake me. I commit the works of my hands into your care. Grant me financial freedom, God to enable me to be a blessing to those around me.
God, I believe you are working things out for my good. I command all demonic hindrances to my financial breakthrough to be totally paralysed in Jesus name.
I possess my possession from the hand of the enemy. I lose myself from every curse of financial bondage. Let all financial hindrances standing my way, be removed.
I declare that I am financially free in Jesus name. I am no longer a slave to poverty.
Thank you, God, for granting me financial freedom.

Thank you Thank you Thank you. It is done. It is done. It is done. I love you God.

3 days: 3AM Prayer for Life

Heavenly father, I come before you today asking for your Divine breakthrough in my life. I believe that you will step into every situation that I am facing

today. Please show Yourself Strong in my life, I
believe you can fix whatever I am going through in
this life. I declare your breakthroughs in my life.

Open doors of new opportunities for me so that I
will be successful and prosperous in all that I do. I
break free from every demonic hold over my life. I
destroy every Satanic hold over my destiny. I ask
for breakthroughs from poverty and diseases. I
declared that I am more than a conqueror in Christ
Jesus. I break free from unfruitfulness and bad
luck. I declare that nothing can stop me from
achieving my goals. Lord, please fill my life with
testimonies and breakthroughs. Nothing can stop
me from achieving my aim in this world.

Fill me afresh with the Wonder of your love and
power. Lord, let your will and promises for my life
come to fulfilment. I come against every arrow and
trap that has been set against my life. I pray, Lord
and Scatter every evil plot of the wicked against my
life. Direct my path, Lord and Lead me in the right
direction. I pray you to lead me to people necessary
for bringing breakthrough into my life.

Beautify my life with your goodness and mercy.
Father Lord, please make me a blessing to my
family and my generation. Anoint my head with oil
and let my cup runneth over. I declare testimonies
in my life, Lord. I am thankful that you will turn
things around for my good.

I am blessed and highly favoured. Lord, your word in James chapter 1 verse 12 says that blessed is the man who remains steadfast under trial for when he has stood the test. He will receive the Crown of Life which God has promised to those who love him. Help me to be patient, amidst the problems I'm facing. I believe Lord that you will always come through for me. Make a way for me where there seems to be none. Renew my mind by the power of your word. I pray you to pull down every stronghold in my life. Your word makes me understand that for the weapon of our Warfare are not carnal, but mighty through God. Break every devour against my finances, Lord. Thank you Lord for your Divine breakthroughs in my life in Jesus mighty name I pray. Amen.

Thank you Thank you Thank you. It is done. It is done. It is done. I love you God.

NOTE: These two prayers do work as I successfully removed my demonic influence from my system and life. Yes, too many people have these influences in their system even though their Ego will acclaim is not true.

4.   THE VSHS PRAYER THERAPY

Veroniqué Salagean Higher Self Prayer Therapy

Talking therapy is great although it's a long endless aftermath of Thinking and Observing your acts. Certainly, I am not against it, however some serious mental and emotional disorders and illnesses run through the genetic lineage (this is recorded as archives in the national health) and all other systems. Some mental issues can be taken out but at the consciousness level only and not from the foundation. Therefore, *VSHS Prayer Therapy has the power to take out any mental, emotional, personality disorders, illnesses and issues from all your systems.*

<u>Note:</u> A while ago, an acquaintance strongly promoted to me The Talking Therapy as being truly helpful. And yes has its own benefits especially if you have in your paradigm the 'time wasting, unbothered and slouching'. Of course I got amused and laughed out loud inside myself as at that point I've had so much life change from my VSHS Prayer Therapy. As for someone truly bothered and aware of their personal development, The Talking Therapy isn't needed.

Do you have anything known of your Mental, Emotional, Personality disorders and illnesses?

How would you describe your childhood, your parents' personalities and people that you've met along your life?

Now, let me present you the VSHS Prayer Therapy:

Prayer works and always! but works wonders on your Faith. *Your Faith plays a major role.* I self-developed and self-mastered this prayer with the help of my Higher Self, Source. It is extremely powerful and the results are permanent, it has proven to me and my life/relationship coach clients. With this prayer I successfully took all my traumas out of my system, freed myself from unnecessary pain and unwanted things. Experimenting or deciding to practise this prayer, you must do *EXACTLY as I tell you to do.*

This prayer is good for taking out unwanted things from your system or tearing contracts with family members or with unwanted people in your life. In the same prayer you have to mention to heal the past lives relationships with that person that you tear the contract with and forgive each other and also take out each other from the full system (I will give an example of this writing below).
With family members or anything that is seen traumas/issues/addictions trace within the family,

you have to mention in the prayer 'take out from my genetic lineage'.

Moreover, I've realised that many are struggling at the moment with Any Type of FEAR, sex addiction, woman addiction, man addiction, narcissism, toxicity, borderline personality disorder, mental and emotional disorders and illness, aggression, abandon, loss, loneliness, rejection, begging, neglect, betrayal, jealousy, anger, revenge, low self-esteem, low self-worth, poor self-image, pornography, prostitution, sluts, cheating, unfaithfulness, disloyalty etc. - so, **you can take out ANYTHING from all your past lives, genetic lineage, energetic system, health system, space, mind and life, these traumas/issues that don't serve you anymore.**

NOTE: A client asked me one time, how did I know what to take out from my system? - I was paying attention to my reality, what was presenting to me and people's traits (all that came towards me without asking). Then, I was googling where the cause of these traits was found. Then I had a name for the issue, illness (being the effect). For example, constant lying and excess self-adoration was Narcissism or behaving and assuming multiple characters was Borderline Personality Disorder.

Furthermore, if you are going through a breakup, with this prayer you can take that person out of your whole system, space, mind and life. Also, you can pray for anyone in your life or in the world as long as you know how they look, who the person is and know the name - who are you praying for? So, in the prayer moment link with that person in your mind as you are praying on their behalf.

To conclude, this might sound out of this world, but the *Prayer is done in the bathroom*. The bathroom is a symbol of cleansing, a holy space where one leaves residues and washes off negativity through the shower. *Keep it to yourself, no need for anybody to know.* So, in the bathroom, close the toilet first, then the bathroom door and find a place towards the Sunrise (East) or where your Intuition tells you (but I do it towards Sunrise, East).

Certainly, I don't suggest facing the toilet or the door, best facing the corner otherwise.

Lay down a mat for your knees (always use a mat, clean folded towel or something comfortable for your knees). Kneeling, prayer posture is a posture of humble feeling that I find to be helping the process. *Close your eyes and take 3 breaths, In, through the nose and Out, through the month and, go inside yourself, connect to your inner Faith, praying inside yourself, then start the prayer with a lower tone voice. Do not rush in saying the prayer, time up well, start 2 minutes prior to the fasting start time.* The repetition of the number three times is an amplifier and the Three Breaths Technique opens the portal towards Divine Power.

When time comes to close the prayer, follow the same steps. Please, respect what you write into the prayer as fasting!

And, *always for any new prayer, write it on an A5 piece of paper first*, then pray it and after the 3 days prayer completion, put it through the paper shredder.

<u>NOTE</u>: I found some people have concerns that this prayer interferes with their religion. Sincerely, the act of fasting is found all around as a sacred practice and God is only one, therefore it's the Ego that sees it into a variation of names and gives meanings that of interference. In this case, I send people to therapy in person since they are not ready for their life change. Talking Therapy is a very long, endless process that alleviates your pain/problem/situation for a while and if one is lucky and blessed, eventually they mature and are ready for the VSHS Prayer. This is an equation that I've found as a repeating human pattern.

Another thing I would like to mention just for your knowledge, with white magic you can undo black magic however, that doesn't mean having a protection around you. And myself from being cursed under white magic, (people claiming that they work with angels) is still an interference of some spirits' energy (might be the giant's souls). It's just that when it comes from God/Universe/Divine Power there is a delay in the deliveries and gratitude involved. Whereas, with black or white magic the deliveries involve revenge, persuasion, are very quick jobs, skyrocket results immediately (one pays this through their health I've realised).

<u>The VSHS Prayer Therapy (this is an example for removing any type of curse and magic before the protection. I cleansed my system first then added any type of protection):</u>

<u>3 days: 00:00 - 12 PM (no food but only water)</u> *OR*
<u>3 days: 6 - 9 PM (no food and no water)</u>
God, please forgive all my sins. I cleanse myself of all misery and sins now.
God, I enter into your presence now because I want you to take out from my all past lives, genetic lineage, health system, energetic system, space, mind and life any type of curse, bad eye, evil eye, magic, hindrances and bad luck. So, I do this fasting for you to help me in this situation.
I put my life in your hands and trust you to take out from my all past lives, genetic lineage, health system, energetic system, space, mind and life any type of curse, bad eye, evil eye, magic, hindrances and bad luck.
I start my fasting now at 6 in the afternoon on the first day/second day/third day with no food and no water and give you my fasting at 9 this evening.

(Affirm continuing with closed eyes) Thank You
Thank You Thank you. It Is Done. It Is Done. It Is
Done.

<u>NOTE:</u> My Ego sees bad eye as spiritual form and
evil eye as material form, hence why I mention both
variations.

**<u>The VSHS Prayer Therapy (this is an example
for putting protection around you or your child -
I've realised people, children are not protected
with so many favourable spirits energy and
black magic performers in the society):</u>**

<u>3 days: 00:00 - 12 PM (no food but only water)</u> *OR*
<u>3 days: 6 - 9 PM (no food and no water)</u>
God, please forgive all my sins. I cleanse myself of
all misery and sins now.
God, I enter into your presence now because I want
you to put around my whole system, space, mind
and life a protection to protect me from any type of
curse, evil eye, bad eye, magic, hindrances and
danger *OR* a powerful protection to block out any
type of takers. So, I do this fasting for you to help
me in this situation.
I put my life in your hands and trust you to put
around my whole system, space, mind and life a
protection to protect me from any type of curse, evil
eye, bad eye, magic, hindrances and danger *OR* a
powerful protection to block out any type of takers.

I start my fasting now at 6 in the afternoon on the
first day/second day/third day of three days with no
food and no water and give you my fasting at 9 this
evening.

(Affirm continuing with closed eyes) Thank You
Thank You Thank you. It Is Done. It Is Done. It Is
Done.

**The VSHS Prayer Therapy (this is an example
for taking out something that doesn't serve you
anymore):**

3 days: 00:00 - 12 PM (no food but only water) *OR*
3 days: 6 - 9 PM (no food and no water)
God, please forgive all my sins. I cleanse myself of
all misery and sins now.
God, I enter into your presence now because I want
you to take out from my all past lives, genetic
lineage, health system, energetic system, space,
mind and life any type of personality disorders and
borderline personality disorder *OR* any type of
mental and emotional disorders and illnesses *OR*
any type of narcissism and aggression *OR* any type
of woman addiction, sex addiction, pornography
and prostitution. So, I do this fasting for you to help
me in this situation.
I put my life in your hands and trust you to take out
from my all past lives, genetic lineage, health

system, energetic system, space, mind and life any type of personality disorders and borderline personality disorder *OR* any type of mental and emotional disorders and illnesses *OR* any type of narcissism and aggression *OR* any type of woman addiction, sex addiction, pornography and prostitution.
I start my fasting now at 12 midnight on the first day/second day/third day of three days with no food but only water and give you my fasting at 12 noon time.

(Affirm continuing with closed eyes) Thank You Thank You Thank you. It Is Done. It Is Done. It Is Done.

The VSHS Prayer Therapy (this is an example for tear contracts with family members):

3 days: 00:00 - 12 PM (no food but only water) *OR*
3 days: 6 - 9 PM (no food and no water)
God, please forgive all my sins. I cleanse myself of all misery and sins now.
God, I enter into your presence now because I want you to heal all my past lives relationships with my material family members, to forgive each other, tear our contracts and take each other out from our genetic lineage, health system, energetic system, space, mind and life. So, I do this fasting for you to help me in this situation.

I put my life in your hands and trust you to heal all my past lives relationships with my material family members, to forgive each other, tear our contracts and take each other out from our genetic lineage, health system, energetic system, space, mind and life.

(Affirm continuing with closed eyes) Thank You Thank You Thank you. It Is Done. It Is Done. It Is Done.

NOTE: Some people judge the tearing contracts with family members however, not everyone has a good or harmonious family.
Doing this prayer, I've realised how much I am into my family members and how much they are into me. Literally we coexist within each other (Why some people say: *Family is important. Family is the most important. Family comes first.* - Now I understand why!)
This prayer about genetic/material family members has shown me in the dream the persons that I have contracts with, which in my case have been only 3 people. Write down in the morning who they are (although you may know) and then you can do the same prayer style for each person individually.
I personally think this prayer is extremely beneficial as I had the experience of family members to stop having a problem with me. Also, I've observed they matured and became more aware of their behaviours and talks. I didn't feel guilty doing it

after so many years of unapologetic headaches, drama and troublemaking from them.

<u>The VSHS Prayer Therapy (this is an example for taking someone out from your life after a breakup - it's fair to take each other out mutually):</u>

<u>3 days: 00:00 - 12 PM (no food but only water)</u> *OR*
<u>3 days: 6 - 9 PM (no food and no water)</u>
God, please forgive all my sins. I cleanse myself of all misery and sins now.
God, I enter into your presence now because I want you to heal all my past lives relationships with ...... (person's name), to forgive each other, tear our contract and take each other out from our all past lives, genetic lineage, health system, energetic system, space, mind and life. So, I do this fasting for you to help me in this situation.
I put my life in your hands and trust you to heal all my past lives relationships with ...... (person's name), to forgive each other, tear our contract and take each other out from our all past lives, genetic lineage, health system, energetic system, space, mind and life.
I start my fasting now at 12 midnight on the first day/second day/third day of three days with no food but only water and give you my fasting at 12 noon time.

(Affirm continuing with closed eyes) Thank You Thank You Thank you. It Is Done. It Is Done. It Is Done.

NOTE: If you are meeting the person again after doing this prayer, you will link yourself again to he/she. Therefore, you will have to do this prayer again. Always listen to your Intuition of what you should do. Also, I've found it is best to do this prayer before breaking up verbally as the process will be smoother for both sides and painless. If for example, after doing this prayer the other person keeps linking telepathically, it might be because of holding onto their items or that person performs some sort of magic (this I've found to be true). You can always do another round and set your strong intention into the desired outcome. Of course if there is a marriage business involved, you should mention within the prayer to keep that part only. You can even make a prayer for a smooth and amicable divorce where you remain in a good co-parenting relationship for the children. You can even restore the respect and joy, love within the marriage, but make sure you ALWAYS in ANY Prayer **forgive each other** and **heal your past lives relationships**. You see, anything can be formulated as you wish, as long as you listen to your Intuition - do as it says and respect the fasting process also the opening and closing the prayer exactly as I tell you.

<u>**The VSHS Prayer Therapy (this example is for
taking out all the past boyfriends/girlfriends and
past male/female relationships - this is because
especially females carry in their systems all the
past relationships; it is said to be the main
reason why historically a Prince/future King had
to marry a virgin girl)**</u>

<u>3 days: 00:00 - 12 PM (no food but only water)</u> *OR*
<u>3 days: 6 - 9 PM (no food and no water)</u>
God, please forgive all my sins. I cleanse myself of
all misery and sins now.
God, I enter into your presence now because I want
you to take out from my all past lives, genetic
lineage, health system, energy system, space,
mind and life all my past boyfriends/girlfriends and
all my past male/female relationships. So, I do this
fasting for you to help me in this situation.
I put my life in your hands and trust you to take out
from my all past lives, genetic lineage, health
system, energy system, space, mind and life all my
past boyfriends/girlfriends and all my past
male/female relationships.
I start my fasting now at 6 in the afternoon on the
first day/second day/third day of three days with no
food and no water and give you my fasting at 9 this
evening.

(Affirm continuing with closed eyes) Thank You
Thank You Thank you. It Is Done. It Is Done. It Is
Done.

NOTE: I think there is nothing wrong with doing this
prayer especially if you plan a serious, pure, divine
marriage/unity. What I've realised is that one
becomes pure and virgin after this prayer. You
simply purify. The prayer is designed to take out all
the entanglements especially from your health
system and energetic system which are one of the
most important aspects.

**The VSHS Prayer Therapy (this is an example
for cleansing your house of negativity, malefic
and demonic energy and putting protection
around it):**

3 days: 00:00 - 12 PM (no food but only water) *OR*
3 days: 6 - 9 PM (no food and no water)
God, please forgive all my sins. I cleanse myself of
all misery and sins now.
God, I enter into your presence now because I want
you to take out from this house any type of
negativity, malefic and demonic energy. Please fill
this house with divine alignment OR ....
(anything you wish) and put a powerful protection

around this house to block out any type of malefic, magic and demonic energy. So, I do this fasting for you to help me in this situation.
I put my life in your hands and trust to take out from this house any type of negativity, malefic and demonic energy. Please fill this house with divine alignment OR ………… (anything you wish) and put a powerful protection around this house to block out any type of malefic, magic and demonic energy.
I start my fasting now at 6 in the afternoon on the first day/second day/third day of three days with no food and no water and give you my fasting at 9 this evening.

(Affirm continuing with closed eyes) Thank You Thank You Thank you. It Is Done. It Is Done. It Is Done.

Make sure you eat very well and stay well hydrated, drinking your daily quantity of water before the prayer.

At 12 PM the next day (after 12 hours of no food but only water) or 9PM (after 3 hours of no food and no water) close the prayer, same procedure as opening it:

God, it is now 9 in the evening (12 noon), I give this fasting to you now with no food and no water and I

Thank You Thank You Thank You for helping me in this situation. It is Done. It is Done. It is Done.

You can eat anything afterwards.

Again at midnight or next day at 6 PM, open the prayer and follow the same procedure for the completion of the three days. <u>Always open and close the prayer so your Higher Self knows what is going on.</u>

<u>NOTE:</u> Out of the prayer hours you can eat anything, no restrictions, however I don't recommend alcohol or any synthetic substance. If you have alcohol or anything lower vibration intake before the prayer, time it well for the system clearing by drinking water for its removal. If you wish your system to update quicker after the prayer(s) I recommend crossing by airplane a patch of water perhaps going on a holiday.

If you wear any energized ring from a Certified Astrologer, you must remove it when you open the prayer and during the prayer hours as I've realised it interferes with the prayer energy. You can wear any jewellery as long as they are not energized.

Another thing, headaches should go away with a coffee maxim 2 intake, otherwise if they only go with nurofen, then who's doing witchcraft on you? Also, just for your knowledge, waking ups during the night out of nowhere is not normal just as things break up suddenly. So, my question is, who visits your spirit during the night? Who visits your house during the night? Or my neighbour's cross road car that its alarm goes off 2,3 times in the afternoon like never before - how come suddenly?

To sum up, what I would actually do is practise some *Quiet The Mind technique for sometime* (start at 10 minutes and increase to 20 minutes as you gain improvement - seated comfortably, spine straight, in Silence, Think Nothing).

Then have a few sessions of KAP, cleanse your system of energy blockages. I will do every two or three weeks one session only when my Intuition tells me to go. Meanwhile, I would work closely with my calendar and appoint some VSHS Prayer Therapy. I would start by taking out from my system *any type of mental and emotional disorders and illnesses.* If you know your mental conditions, you should start with that. Once you open the portal with your Higher Self, the rest of your issues will come out - *they will be presented by others to you and you will instantly know.* Just pay attention to the Signs!

However, I will follow with *borderline personality disorder* then another prayer only for *psychopathy and sociopathy.* It's been presented to me by so many people with serious mental and personality issues, *Narcissism.* Also, common amongst the masses are: *low self-esteem, low self-worth, low self-respect, poor self-image* and *selfishness* and the first ones listed below. Try to write in the prayer maximum of 3, 4 things, but not more at a time.

I've discovered our system is so complex and goes in depth, therefore you will be surprised what is hidden within you. Listen to your *Intuition*, follow your instincts and take action. I've also discovered people have a lot of *neglect, abandon, need for validation, insecurities, betrayal, cheating* and *Any types of Abuse*. The list is so long, I can type so many more things. All of these I successfully took them out from my all system sectors with the VSHS Prayer Therapy (*do EXACTLY as I say for the prayers*).

If you feel you need to change your paradigm / mindset then Psych-K (You take things out with the VSHS Prayer Therapy and put things in with the Psych-K. If you have a serious health issue, then QHHT). Again, follow your Intuition, listen to it, it will take you to the right people of your style and lessons to be learned if you have any. Please keep an open-mind and think of it only as a journey of personal transformation and development for the New Earth moving. I've realised, a lot of *abundance* people require in their paradigm. Abundance is the opposite of Lack.

About QHHT, I would do a session if there is something in your *Health System* that can't happen to be removed through the power of VSHS Prayer Therapy. **QHHT** by Dolores Cannon is a past life regression session with a healing process from your Higher Self. So, in the session you will be able

to release anything unwanted for your desired
outcome.

Moreover, if you feel at times or are invited to go to
Church or people gatherings, please do visit as I've
found there to be presented information about
where you are in your personal journey. *Do pay
attention to the people's testimonies.*

Around us, there are 360 degree signs and
directions just to pay attention. But, if you keep
yourself constantly complaining, being upside
down, with an immature attitude, then you are only
lost in space. *You must be dedicated and
committed if you want to change your life.*

Well, I am very sure there will be an incredible
contrast to many to cause determination and desire
for change. **When you change, Everything
changes!**

Planet Earth comes to completion of its move to a new dimension and frequency, just for the old souls to make the move into it. The volunteer souls have done an incredible job and their contribution is Much Appreciated!

<u>Just for a fun fact:</u> I see in 2025, yes - the volunteer souls and the ones that cleansed their negativity and demonic influence - moving into the New Earth, so society is dividing. But, the ones left into the Old Earth, will all clash with each other including being victims of black and white magic from their fellows. The reason I see this is because I've clashed myself through a personal manifestation in 2024 and also as being a victim of white magic in 2023 (both stories are found in CHANGE YOUR LIFE: with Practical Techniques). Moreover, unknowing at that time, a close friend of mine clashed as well and has been a victim of black magic instead since mid 2023 for a year. Therefore, searching for rescues he realised the actual cause (acknowledgment and awareness that the actual black magic was running through his genetic lineage and hidden inside him - it had an origin). Myself I had quite similar acknowledgment and awareness but through the power of my intuition and protection I have around myself which I was born with. In 2025 perhaps many will die due to the inability to adapt to the New Earth's frequency. And I don't see any war but only this particular clashing with each other into the Old Earth. Some people will continue aging and their issues will show on their face appearance.

AFTERWORD

I would like to Thank You to my beautiful Universe that we co-create with, my beautiful Source, my Higher Self, my whole system, space and mind (at least this is how my Ego sees it at the moment, perhaps not in 10 years from now) for this incredible masterpiece book.

We have now split into two worlds and I've made the move into the New World and am proud of that (I recommend for you to read Dolores Cannon books). I've managed to get to the end of three hells over two and half decades where I took only the good from it all and become who I am today, constantly evolving and advancing. I believe we are living in an incredibly rich Universe and we have the ability to materialise things from thin air, therefore this book I don't see as a threat to the old system (Ego / Material system) of slavery. Since we are living on a material planet, I have no desire to compete with the matrix.

I also believe that this world on Planet Earth will forever have contrast, good and bad and choices (freewill). Certainly, since a vast majority breathes in the ever advancing ego system, this book should not create a threat towards the system.

To sum up, there are so so many things here on Planet Earth, yet to be acknowledged and media published. I truly want the best for everyone and I believe everyone deserves True, Divine Happiness and living Heaven on Earth just like me.